P9-CZV-253

Dorling **DK** Kindersley

LONDON, NEW YORK, SYDNEY, DELHI, PARIS, MUNICH, AND JOHANNESBURG

Written by Angela Royston
Editor Mary Ling
Art Editor Nigel Hazle
Production Marguerite Fenn
Illustrator Rowan Clifford

First American Edition, 2001

00 01 02 03 04 05 10 9 8 7 6 5 4 3 2 1

Published in the United States by Dorling Kindersley Publishing, Inc.
95 Madison Avenue, New York, New York 10016

Copyright © 2001 Dorling Kindersley Limited

All rights reserved under International and Pan-American Copyright Conventions. No part of this publication may be reproduced, stored in a retrieval system, or transmitted in any form or by any means, electronic, mechanical, photocopying, recording or otherwise, without the prior written permission of the copyright owner. Published in Great Britain by Dorling Kindersley Limited.

A CIP catalog record for this book is available
from the Library of Congress

ISBN 0-7894-7654-1

Color reproduction by Scantrans, Singapore
Printed and bound in Italy by L.E.G.O.

See our complete
catalog at

www.dk.com

SEE HOW THEY GROW
CHICK

photographed by
JANE BURTON

A DORLING KINDERSLEY BOOK

WHITING PUBLIC LIBRARY
WHITING. IN 46394

Hatching

This is my mother. She is sitting on her eggs. Inside each egg a chick is growing. One of them is me.

I start to chip around the inside of my eggshell.

I push my shell apart.

At last I am free.

Out of the egg

I am one hour old. My brothers
and sisters have
hatched too.
We are
chirping to
each other.

My feathers have dried
and now they are soft
and downy.

Learning to feed

I am three days old and I am feeling
hungry. My mother is eating seed.
How does she do it?
I watch her
carefully.

I stretch
up and take the seed
from her beak.

It tastes so good
I decide to peck
some myself.

A drink of water

I am eight days old now. New feathers are growing on my wings.

What is Mom doing? She is dipping her beak into a bowl of water.

I hop into the bowl.
The water is cool and wet.
My sister is getting in too.

13

False alarm

I am two weeks old.
Today I am looking
for food with
my mother.

Is something wrong?
My mother is flapping
her wings.
She clucks
at us to run
away.

It is a false alarm.
Nothing is wrong.
Mother calls us
back.

Meeting Dad

I am four weeks old now. I am growing bigger every day.

Here is my father.
Look how big he is!

Dad is very friendly.
He lets me ride on
his back.

Growing bigger

I am eight weeks old and
all my feathers have
grown.

I have a
bright red
comb on
my head and a
red wattle under my beak.

I am big and strong. At last I can look after myself.

I use my beak to keep myself neat and clean. I am proud of my fine feathers.

See how I grew

The egg

One hour old

Three days old

Eight days old

Two weeks old

Four weeks old   Eight weeks old

WHITING PUBLIC LIBRARY
WHITING, IN 46394

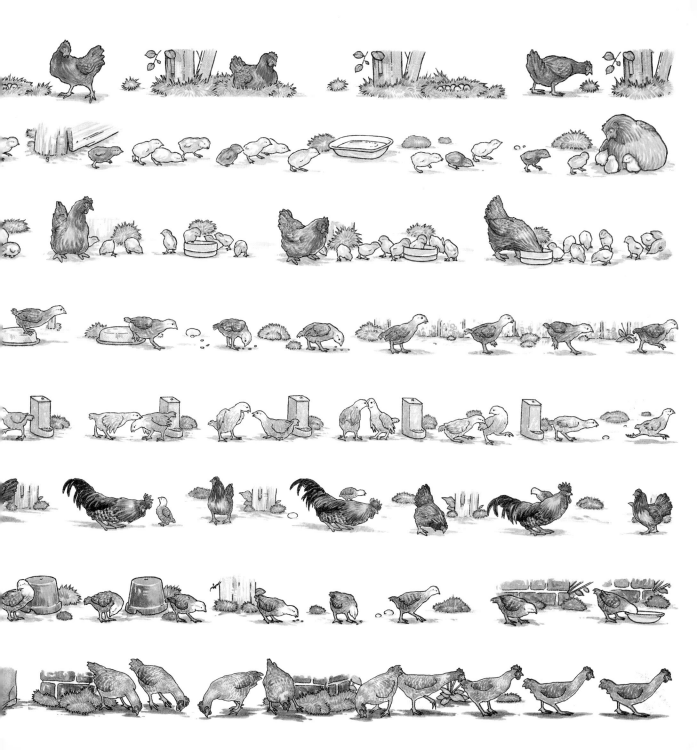